AF347920

THE
FOUR HINGES
OF THE
WORLD

POEMS

Carlos Reyes

Acknowledgments

Some of these poems were first published in *Choeofpleirn Press*, *On the Seawall*, and *The Lake*.

Cover photo *A Wall at Petra* by Karen Checkoway
Author's photo by Sandra E. Williams

The author wishes to acknowledge Karen Checkoway, his first reader, for her work on this volume.

Cyberwit.net
HIG 45 Kaushambi Kunj, Kalindipuram
Allahabad – 211011 (U.P.) India
http://www.cyberwit.net
Tel: +(91) 9415091004
E-mail: info@cyberwit.net

The winds . . . rushed abroad
from the four hinges of the world.

— Milton, *Paradise Regained*

Contents

II
Out of Houston

III
Like the Last Skirling Leaves at Year's End

For the four hinges of my world:

Mike, Amy, Nina & Rachel

I
Flecks

In December When Small Birds Like Black Flecks Before my Eyes Flick Across a Tentative Blanketed Morning

I wake to a few flakes,
delicate, tentative, just

a right amount of expression,
though I am not sure of what.

But they remind me of me
first thing in the morning

without my tea, still
tentative, too, about the morning,

the day, about me, the other
wise dark world.

Still the tentative blue
sky wants to argue its case

before a judge that worries
not about power, knows

it can easily destroy
a snowy morning.

A Year Past of Untangled Threads,
A New Year, Its Foolish Resolutions

— for Edwin Madrid

TODAY I am trapped in my work of poetry
in a spider web of unbreakable tensile silken
strands or winding fibers of sisal ropes
easily imagined as chiding snakes:

TOMORROW the gentle loving squeeze of a boa
will remind me of the worrisome constant urge
I have to write as if I could ever forget.

THE DAY AFTER an anaconda warns me
of writing's strength, its serious nature,
an ever present danger it entails.

The Beard as Timekeeper

Yesterday at the Zoom Seder
I saw my son had grown a beard.

My first thought: it's one
of those stick-on disguises.

But it was white . . . I'd not
seen him in the time

it took him to grow the beard,
the white hair. How dare he

be that old? I shaved my
white beard, it made me look old.

His turned white waiting
for the pandemic to end

for if the hairs on your head
are numbered so must be

those of your beard.
He didn't set to counting them

in his dead time or did he?
Each white hair is a second,

a minute, an hour, a day,
until a year has passed.

The pandemic yet
perches on our shoulder

an eager vulture,
our beards grow long.

Pesach 2021

Happy Valentine's Day

The waiter has escaped,
abandoned the field

The bottle of Dom Perignon
stands a last Centurion between
the two full moon porcelain plates

White linen napkins wrinkled
and discarded like clothing
left behind by lovers before bed,

Two tall menus have fallen tentlike
for a campout beside the two round lakes
or permanent break from the wind

they shelter a crimson message unread

An Event at Mt Vernon

Five gentlemen, wigged and silk
stockinged sit around in sunshine
on a hillock talking amicably
beneath a standing guard

a cumulonimbus cloud.
Ben's shoe is unbuckled only the sun
takes any notice he is dreaming
of flying a kite dangling a key

as though with the help
of a coming storm he will
surprise all the bored talkers
by inventing electricity.

There is a woman, Martha,
lurking at the edge of men.
She disappears suddenly
when the picture slips in its frame

at the first clap of thunder.

Fossil

At exactly 8:30 a.m.
from the Grade School
sweet bells peal out
across the small valley.

Children line up,
the flag pops.

A northwest wind
brings the sun

into a town with no malls,
no fast food, no taxis.

Where the streets study
American sedans
and flatbed pickup trucks.

In the Two Room School

We memorized poems in the heat of a wood furnace:
Under the spreading chestnut, the village smithy stands...
It rang false, was nothing like my grandfather's forge.

We believed little our teacher told us.
The earthquake that rattled our school
knocking a few bricks from the chimney
was a greater power's judgement

on an hysterical teacher who in her panic
herded us down a shaky building's wooden stairs
to recess in a muddy field we called the playground.

In the Schoolyard

Of our up and down two room schoolhouse
there were no oak trees for shade, no grass lawn.
There was mud in winter and spring, dust in the fall
a sopping American flag waving over it all.

We looked out the window at the weeping
willow by the pond. The valley had little else
but high weeds, Scotch thistle along the creek,
Queen Anne's lace rattling in the southwest breeze.

March arctic storms brought snow for weeks.

Youth's Initials

*In Neruda's home on Isla Negra, his carpenter carved
on the rafters the names of illustrious visitors.*

They labored here in Zimmerman's Feed Mill
sacking whatever rushed down the chutes,
never stopped, loaded it on trucks.

In dim light I read those names
carved on the beam above
with a pen knife: Bellwood,

a ringing, sonorous, romantic name
of a boy I knew and was afraid not to like.

Friday night's hero but not mine
though I drank beer with him
out along the river bank.

Small town boys never stopped,
sacrificed to the work ethic
their lives, left names

in mills engraved on old growth timbers.

Rough Times

The pale moon
        a white horse

clambers up from the ditch
        through shattered windows

of a forlorn
        crashed automobile.

Bird Baths

When a paved surface doesn't come up to grade,
leaving depressions that fill with water when it rains,
engineers and surveyors call the puddles "bird baths."

The twenty mallards circle
above the southeast corner

of the empty reservoir twelve times
checking again and again

for the missing water
they left behind in the fall.

Two birds don't trust the flock
can't believe their eyes

finally alight on the pool
dry but for "birdbaths."

They recognize the ramp
where they dried their feathers

in morning sun gathered
ducklings beneath wings to hide them.

None of the others trust
what they fly over.

Only the two ducks from the circling flock
ignore the majority

make their own decision, see for themselves
that however inviting, the "bird baths"

are too shallow to swim in. But
they waddle around, strutting.

They alone brave enough to risk
returning to earth.

Ethnocentrics

He's washing his hands
before he eats (cute, but razor

sharp claws — ask any dog, cat).
But he will wash them

Pandemic or not with nothing at all
going through all the motions

or laves them with dirt or dust
if no water is nearby.

Another possibility:
the raccoon prays

before each meal
and after.

Pilot House

I always wanted a pilot house
atop a sturdy vessel like a tug

but instead I have an office
on the second floor of a Tudor cottage.

It offers little for long range viewing
beyond the play block houses —

there is an extinct volcano
a forested hill but that's all.

I can't rely on an imagination
of x-ray vision but I have dreams.

The most common: rivers
chockablock with boats and ships,

small harbors I never noticed
on maps, or on the coast

coming upon a small haven, stopping
to watch out my windshield

model vessels huddling
in an anchorage, one tenebrous boat

fighting a seething perilous bar.

Even the Thinnest Cloud

I didn't ask for more than a bit of blue in the sky.
— Luis Cernuda

in the cerulean sky blocks the sun
from your eyes, casts doubt, spoils

your most sparkling awakening.
The day is off to a brilliant start, until

marine air invades, covering your world,
causing you to lose confidence in sun's

power to return, burn away yesterday's
old rags, these morning clouds.

Marie Curie

The one dress she owns
is really a smock.

As she slips from the lab
to the kitchen to prepare a meal

you can hear test tubes
of radium tinkling

like small glass bells.
She never leaves radium

it never abandons her, not for
a hundred years, awarding

her a unique immortality.
We'd never risk our lives

for art to that extent,
never allow our work unread

to be buried in lead caskets
untouchable pages,

our precious notebooks.
Our only hope: a glowing light,

a human shape hovering
over us, our unfinished work.

As Winter Comes

The custom is to close the drapes
at sunset and open them at dawn
but in the eighteen years I've lived

on this street I have never seen
the drapes on the salt box
across the street open until today.

Suddenly the picture window's drapes
are flung open as though it were spring
time to let in winter's weak light.

Neighborly gossip says someone
across the street is dying they've placed
his bed in the living room, arranged

so he can look out to the south
catch sight of whatever is coming.

These days the drapes are never closed
day or night, though there's little
difference in light these foreshortened

days when total darkness arrives
mid afternoon and the saltbox
becomes a brilliant light

house to guide whatever ship
is coming on the south wind.

The crows in my front yard
are digging up the moss, searching
for acorns the squirrels buried.

They pay no attention to the
reflections off the big picture window.
The dying man can't see them

when they suddenly take flight,
fragments of silky blackness. Evaporating
clouds patch the sky blue

bring a subtle light change.
The open drapes allow darkness
in or rays as faint as odors to

escape. The man in bed across the street:
somebody's brother he was. A wake

leaves all the candles burning
through the night.

Poem After a Line by Emily Dickinson

"Departure from the hinge"

Departing from the hinge.

Departing from the house.

Departing from the morning
into midday and midnight

Departing from the hinge

the door you closed finally
swung from.

The leather hinge
on the barn door

dried after fifty years
and cracked leaving

a corner of
the door hanging onto nothing
but air

and no one
there to repair
it. Your life
all despair
when you, like the door,

depart from the hinge.

How I Am Confident in Medical Science

Just before I go into
cataract surgery

the nurse asks
would you like

the doctor to pray?
No, but

on second thought
I'll take

that tranq
you offered earlier.

Passport

I.
I know the obvious definition of passport
but I translate it as "coming through the door,"
or more precisely coming through the birth canal
into life from my safe private sea to a rocky shore:

A short trip that almost kills my mother
if you ask her, because of the size of my head.
I'm not sure if she actually tells me that
or if a sibling or relative divulges it.

This particular badly focused
memory stays with me for 80 years
as though my mother needs to keep
reminding me of her life.

Whether she tells me that, whether
it is true or false is not important
this story is firmly lodged like

a grain of sand in the oyster.
in my head: that big trunk of memories.

It seeps through with all the stories
I hear as a child. The trouble with memory:
We're never sure if it is a thing we experienced
or anecdote someone tells us.

II.
But I am through the door into my life.

III.
Then a door slams.

Winter wind whistles in, my father
staggers toward me in
a wave of moonshine alcohol,
crashes into my high chair, sending it,

me sprawling across a cold
unforgiving kitchen floor.

Hot Tamales

During blackouts
keeping our window
shades down at night
was not real, nor bombers

coming all the way
from Germany targeting
a tenement here in middle
America in 1943.

Carbon arc searchlights
sweeping summer sky
for enemy planes, night
not real but the tamale man

misplaced, was, pushing
a cart through gritty shadows
singing "Red hot tamales."
As I look back, tamales

on North Campbell were
as unlikely as air raids,
bombers roaring above
flying through klieg lights.

The aroma a memory
of fresh corn tamales
to this thin day rises through
the years like steam.

The Odds: An Osage Orange in a Botanical Garden, Marnay-Sur-Seine

— for Chris Howell

In a windy afternoon
on the high plains of Kansas
you showed me an Osage Orange.
More like a hand grenade

than a fruit, not edible
though the Osage might
have been driven to try it
in times of famine. But

they fashioned bows and
arrows from its durable wood.
In a rustic garden
4,800 miles across the

North Atlantic from
the American prairie
I am contemplating once again
that pitchy fruit, pondering

who carried it here, some
thing of no apparent value,
not beautiful but an oddity,
planted it on the banks

of a river more melancholy
than the Neosho, the Seine,
that flows through a village
much smaller than Emporia

where I first saw the Osage Orange:
its name poetic, but in reality
green and knobby, misnamed
and like me a lost traveler.

II
Out of Houston

Out of Houston

— for Karen

Over the gulf we flew
a hundred miles off course

to avoid
the hurricane.

As lightning opened
our way through the sky

off the wingtip flashes
pulses, love's messages

left me thinking of you
until I fell asleep

still kissing you
all the way to Bogotá

all the way
to the top of the Andes.

Panecillo

At the middle of the world
a small boy pees happily
from the curb on the chrome
of a parked new Japanese car,
somehow adding a luster
matched only by
his eyes, rays of the sun
nowhere the intimidating father
or mother shadow over him
from the sidewalk, nor
does the looming cloud
of poverty detract from
his obvious pleasure in that act.

At the Mosaic Cafe

– for Edwin, Aleyda and Anaís

Here pitched out over the city
watching the colonial bullring below...
The immutable division between night and day
is not a great cup that refills itself

in a morning of light then empties
at night—nor is a struggle
between goodness and evil,
but a quiet drama in which

the two main characters
know perfectly their roles
and with precision carry them out:

One leaving punctually the scene
while the other arriving, begins
to turn on all the lights and stars of Quito.

On the Way to Lake Cuicocha

The woven woolen strands
are suddenly taut across the road.

Whoever drives it, this car is new
and the road dead ends, goes only to the lake.

They stop us, then quickly drop
the weak line, long since discarded

as a tether for goats, thin cords
spliced and knotted together

abandoned *quipus* that might as well
be spider webs sparkling

in the last hopeful sunrays
the day disappearing in Andean mist.

Those who line the road stop us —
their temporary barricade lasts

long enough for their hands clasped
in supplication to reach out

for the driver to roll down the window
offer a few *Sucres*, a pitiful and optional toll,

but not long enough for the wind and rain
our consciences to smite us.

As though we expected — instead of gentle
hands outstretched — bandits from behind

eucalyptus trees, swarming out
onto the pot-holed road to surround us.

We quickly roll up our window, shield
against the cold afternoon, the faces,

prayerful hands, upturned palms that hold
no more than the bubble of the world.

Abalone on the Beach

Esmeraldas, Ecuador is Africa,
except the language here is Spanish.

Sand and wind, the oldest colonizers,
retake the town.

The three-wheel bicycle rickshaws
try to conquer the sand drifted
into dunes along the main street.

There's a bar just above high tide,
it's a few short steps from the sun
and waves, to a drink.

South along the beach
the old lighthouse is dark
but fisherman use the tower's
silhouette as a guide
even if the lamp is out,
to find port, where they

bring their *cayucos* up onto the sand.
in early afternoon — well away
from the tourists swimming in the sea
or hiding under beach umbrellas —
to string their catch, dump
seawater from their boats,
pull them up above high tide.

In straw hat and cutoffs, a man
sits in the sand, pries open an abalone,

chops it into pieces with a rusty machete,
serves it raw in the shell for fifty cents.

Whatever he puts on
for seasoning, it smells of the sea,
has the flavor of rusty metal,
the taste of Africa.

Caribbean Nocturne

As we pull away from the dock
in San Juan, past

San Felipe del Morro
the Southern Cross

overhead pursues me South
out through the Caribs's sea.

I leave the darkness
go below to a feverish dream

drummed into me
by the throb of an engine

the ship's heart, in a night
whose following morning is flying

fish swept from the deck.

III
Like the Last Skirling Leaves at Year's End

Remembering Emma on This Dark Oregon Day

More than two decades ago
you went to Brazil drawn by
the rhythm of sambas.
Today here without you
our sky has shrunk
leaving us as they say in Ireland
under a closed sky.
Blankets of low clouds
keep us from light
hide from our ears
the rush of planes,
birdsong, the day's music.
We're left with dim promises
of light returning on a day
when the sun leaves us at 9 p.m.
In the morning I expect
to be awakened to find
Orfeo on my stoop
strumming his guitar. He knows
exactly the golden notes necessary
to tempt back your light.

A Walrus in the Wall

A child hides a tuskless walrus in the wall
its button one eye hanging by a thread

excelsior stuffing coming from a belly
torn open by clawing, desperate rats.

The slate cracked down the middle, a child's
ABCs chalk mixed with dust and cobwebs

before the story of a family was told:
A history I ignored when I tore into the lath

and plaster wall for a supposed remodel
of my existence, oblivious to any story but my own.

The childhood hidden in the walls
of the century old house was not mine.

Little did I care for people who lived there
but I kept the walrus, a talisman on my desk

through winter storms and break up
of ice on rivers, marriages

abandoned in dark corners of rentals.
With all my vagabondage

an ark of books was lost
after the flood in a basement.

In my absence a landlord
taking it for unpaid rent expecting

a treasure there found only moldering
poetry magazines and books he took

to the city dump. It was years before
I realized in my jumping from bed to bed

from house to house the treasure I lost.
Until one day I turned to re-examine my life:

that last piece of history, the walrus is gone.
I could not imagine I left it aground

on a far shore, buried beneath
a tide of debris of years.

Jackie

An organ grinder
occasionally wanders
through my childhood.

In a small cage
a little red fez lies
in the corner, the
embroidered jacket hangs

from a miniature hanger.
A frayed rope trails
through the door.

The bent man, mustaches
glowing silver
cranks the hurdy gurdy.

He himself has to pass
around the tin cup
to an indifferent murder

of crows who on hearing
the Tarantella fly down
to see the capuchin,
Giacomino or Jackie.

When they see no monkey,
realize the cup is empty

they fly back to their rookery.
After seven decades, across
prairies, snowy mountains echo
faint notes of a Tarantella.

Canon

In our libraries
we measure the thickness

of our poetry books
with calipers.

Though spineless they
are courageous.

A Poem

is a stick
of dynamite.

Light its fuse
it scatters

particles
of words to the

four hinges
of your world.

Novel for the End of the Year

The atheist
nibbles on the body of Christ

The way a comet nibbles
on goldfish wafers

A Summing Up

On my dead-end street
they call my place

the poet's house

In my view
like Dickinson

I dwell in the possibility
that it is truly
a fairer house than prose

Recent Books by Carlos Reyes

Osage Elegy (2021)

The Ebbing Tide (2021)

Lament for Us All (2021)

Sea Smoke to Ashes (2020)

The Keys to the Cottage: Stories from the West of Ireland (2015)

Along the Flaggy Shore, (2018)

Guilt in Our Pockets: Poems from South India (2017)